DIRECTOR
NOTEBOOK
for FILMMAKERS

Belongs to:

© XT Media Books

If you like this book, please consider leaving a review on Amazon.
Thank you.

di·rec·tor

A person who supervises the actors, camera crew, and other staff for a movie, play, television program, or similar production.

Made in the USA
Las Vegas, NV
29 December 2023

83672466R00069